MW01173960

FOCUSED

(Follow Ones Course Until Successful Every Day)

DEONTE MOSS

FOCUSED

ISBN: 9798987671801

Book Cover by: Deonte Moss

Email: deontemoss@gmail.com

Formatting & Editing by: Pieces of Me LLC

Number: 419-322-0438

Email: sixtysecondspark@gmail.com

Introduction

Life can be a lot like school. You learn by listening and asking questions. The people around you provide a tremendous resource. They have experiences and knowledge that you do not have, and you have an opportunity to learn from them. If you have surrounded yourself with people who have no desire to grow or increase and are not interested in helping you in that pursuit, this is the time to evaluate your associations. Find people who can teach you. Ask

questions. Then, listen closely to what they say. Seek to understand. Make a goal to learn something new every day that will benefit you in reaching your own goals and dreams. If you do this, you will be amazed at how much your mind will increase and your thinking will expand in just a few weeks. "Give a Man a Fish, and You Feed Him for a Day. Teach a Man To Fish, and You Feed Him for a Lifetime."

#focused

(follow ones course until successful everyday)

DAY 1:

If you really want to do something, you will find away. If you don't, you will find an excuse.

DAY 2:

NO ONE CAN HURT YOU WITHOUT YOUR CONSENT.

DAY 3:

I don't care what anybody has to say about me, ESPECIALLY IF IT'S NOT TRUE.

DAY 4:

Divorce Your Story And Marry The Truth.

DAY 5:

One Of My Biggest Mistakes In Life Is Thinking People Will Show Me The Same Love That I've Shown Them.

DAY 6:

Many people love the idea of you but lack the maturity to handle the reality of you.

DAY 7:

The strongest people are not those who show strength in front of us but those who win battles we know nothing about.

DAY 8:

A relationship is like a house, if a lightbulb goes out, you fix the lightbulb.

You don't go buy a new house.

DAY 9:

Sometimes you block your blessings by telling everyone your business.

DAY 10:

I wanted to give up on GOD a few times. I felt things didn't go my way, but I loved GOD through it. GOD always made a way.

THIS IS A LESSON ON UNCONDITIONAL LOVE.

DAY 11:

Trying to change the past will only hurt your future.

Day 12:

Some Days You Just Have To CREATE Your Own SUNSHINE.

Day 13:

You don't get to choose when or who you meet,

but

you do get to choose who you hold on to.

Day 14:

"I always write 'WAKE UP', on my to-do list, so I can at least accomplish one thing a day."

Day 15:

Stay out of your feelings, ain't no money in there.

DAY 16:

They can’t see who you are because they are looking for who you were.

DAY 17:

Some people want it to happen. Some wish it would happen. Others make it happen.

DAY 18:

Sometimes We're Tested, Not To Show Our Weaknesses, But To Discover Our Strengths.

Day 19:

How come when you catch somebody lying, they be madder than you?

Day 20:

Don't trust people who don't love themselves and tell you, "I love you." There is an African proverb that says: "Be careful when a naked person offers you a shirt."

Day 21:

Don't Worry!

Don't Waste Your Time.

GOD Knows Everything.

GOD Is In Control.

Day 22:

Have you ever felt like the people you sacrificed for the most don't appreciate it?

-Jesus Christ

Day 23:

Sometimes You Just Need to Cancel Your Subscription to People's Issues.

Day 24:

It's not the devil. It's YOU!

Day 25:

When Your Past Calls,

Don't Answer.

It Has Nothing New To Say.

Day 26:

It's funny how when in school, you're taught a lesson, then given a test, but in life, it seems you're given a test that teaches you a lesson.

Day 27:

Your setback is a setup for your comeback!

Day 28:

Not Everyone You Lose Is A Loss.

Day 29:

Don't wander away from yourself to get closer to someone else.

Day 30:

Most Accidents Don't Stop Traffic.

Most Accidents Stop Because People Stop To See Them.

Day 31:

ANOTHER DAY. ANOTHER OPPORTUNITY.

Day 32:

If you got something good, hold on to it.

Day 33:

He Told Her, "If The Caterpillar Gave Up The Fight, It Would Never Take Flight!"

Press In, Aim High, and Find Your Inner Butterfly.

Day 34:

If you keep Winning, some will hate you.

Day 35:

If You Ever Get Caught Sleeping On The Job, Slowly Raise Your Head and Say, "In Jesus' Name, Amen."

Day 36:

The Person you care for the most is the person you'll let hurt you the most.

Day 37:

We sit on

million-dollar

talents

to make

$17 an hr.

They Pay us

to forget our

dreams.

Day 38:

It's Not What You Get Your Kids That Makes Them Great, It's What You Leave In Them.

Day 39:

A Wise Man Once Said:

"If You Find Yourself In A Hole, The Worst Thing You Can Do Is Keep Digging."

Day 40:

I Believe CHARACTER Is The Real Foundation Of SUCCESS.

It's Not Money, Position, or Power.

Day 41:

It's not always easy to stand for what you believe in especially when it means standing alone.

Day 42:

Don't lose your queen bee Chasing a butterfly and end up with a roach.

LET US SPRAY!

Day 43:

You cannot heal in the same environment where you got sick.

Day 44:

You wanting a sign is a sign.

Day 45:

WARNING:
Reflections in the mirror may be distorted
by
socially constructed ideas of beauty.

Day 46:

When You Do Something You Love, It's Never Work.

DAY 47:

PRAY

AND

PREPARE!

Day 48:

You don't become what you want, you become what you believe.

Day 49:

When I was in school, on really cold days, we used to walk backward to school.

Day 50:

WE ARE ALL BEING JUDGED BY SOMEONE WHO ISN'T EVEN CLOSE TO HAVING THEIR STUFF TOGETHER!

Day 51:

If a Man wants to find a Real Woman, He has to become a Real Man. Women are not excluded it goes hand in hand.

Day 52:

It's totally okay to say "You know what, this isn't making me happy" and to walk away from whatever or whoever is keeping you from your happiness.

Day 53:

A society that hides cures just to gain profits from medication, is the definition of the root of all evil.

Day 54:

Passion Is Energy.

Feel The Power That Comes From Focusing On What Excites You.

Day 55:

Sometimes Failure is only there to point you in the right direction.

Day 56:

Forgiveness is giving up the Hope that things could have been different.

Day 57:

I Am Not Defined By My Mother's and Father's Mistakes.

Instead, I use it as Fuel for My Success Today.

DAY 58:

A bird sitting on a tree is never afraid of the branch breaking because its trust is not in the branch

but in its wings.

Day 59:

Stop Giving The Same Person Different Opportunities To Disappoint You.

Day 60:

You Don't Have To Build A Relationship With Everyone You've Forgiven.

Day 61:

They never tell the whole story, only the part that makes you look bad.

Day 62:

Accept What Cannot Be Changed.

Day 63:

Most People Will Choose A Familiar Misery Over A Foreign Happiness.

Day 64:

Make a habit of shutting down conversations that involve hating on other people.

Day 65:

There Are 1,440 Minutes In A Day Use Some For Yourself.

Day 66:

The cruelest lies are often told In silence.

DAY 67:

Every Man Has Two Options:

1.) Stand Up and be the MAN she needs You to be.

2.) Sit Down so She can see the MAN behind You.

DAY 68:

People say "you don't know what you've got until it's gone."

That’s not always true. They knew, they just didn't think they'd lose You.

DAY 69:

No One Ever Got Rich Working A 9-to-5.

DAY 70:

if I text you at

8:10

you are supposed to reply at

8:09.

DAY 71:

Sleep doesn't help, if it's your Soul that's tired.

DAY 72:

The first thing you should know about me is that I am not you.

A lot more will make sense after that.

DAY 73:

SUCCESS depends on the second letter.

DAY 74:

Sometimes Getting Unfriended in life is Amazing.

DAY 75:

LIVE YOUR LIFE SO FOLKS WON'T HAVE TO LIE AT YOUR FUNERAL!

DAY 76:

A BETTER ME

IS

COMING...

DAY 77:

I don't think Black Boys need to be rescued.

I believe they need to be Empowered.

DAY 78:

HEALTHY SELF!

HEAL

THY

SELF!

DAY 79:

Haters will broadcast your failure and whisper your success.

DAY 80:

G.O.A.L.S
GOD
OVERSEES
ALL
LOVE
STORIES!

DAY 81:

Don't waste your time entertaining individuals that Harriet Tubman would have shot!

Day 82:

Love doesn't need to be perfect, It just has to be true.

Day 83:

GOD

First!

Day 84:

No Relationship Is Worth Sacrificing Your Dignity Or Self-Respect.

Day 85:

What You Think You Are Worthy Of Is What You Attract.

You Change Your Reality When You Change Your Mentality.

Day 86:

One Thing I Can't Stand Is A Liar, Especially In My Face And I Know The Truth.

Day 87:

A Hypocrite is someone who is mad at someone for something they do. Don't be a Hypocrite.

Day 88:

Circumstances Do NOT Make A Man, They Reveal Him.

Day 89:

If they hadn't told me I was ugly, I never would have searched for my beauty. And if they hadn't tried to break me down, I wouldn't know that I'm unbreakable.

Day 90:

Some Of The Darkest Pasts, Make The Brightest Futures. Let Go Of Who You Were & Step Into The Light Of Who You ARE.

Day 91:

MY GOD

IS

AN

AWESOME GOD!

Day 92:

DO NOT LIMIT WHAT IS UNLIMITED TO YOU!

Day 93:

Do not buy where you will not be hired.

Day 94:

Sometimes You Just Have To Support Yourself.

Day 95:

Sometimes,
What you are
going through
is
your fault.

Day 96:

Knowledge is POWER. No Matter where You Heard, Read, or Saw it... Except It!

Day 97:

What do you want to be? What does GOD tell you to be? 2 different questions!

Day 98:

Someone made up dinosaur noises without even hearing them.

Day 99:

Why Do We Have Noses That Run And Feet That Smell?

Day 100:

FELLAS, STOP GIVING YOUR BODY TO WOMEN WHO DON'T WANT TO PUT A RING ON IT.

Know your worth...

Day 101:

Every Saint Has

A

Past.

Every Sinner Has

A

Future.

Day 102:

LIFE DOESN'T GET EASIER, WE JUST BECOME STRONGER!

Day 103:

Fellas you put the toilet seat down for her but ask yourself,

when has she

left it up

for you?

Know Your Worth!

Day 104:

Imagine getting NO support then BOOM, You're a MILLIONAIRE!

Day 105:

You never know
how long
something you say
will stay

In

a person's mind.

Day 106:

Your Beliefs Don't Make You A Better Person, Your Behavior Does.

Day 107:

Make it a Great Day.

Day 108:

STOP LEAVING OUT THE PART OF THE STORY WHERE YOU MESSED UP!

Day 109:

The Quickest Way To Get Someone's Attention Is To No Longer Want It.

Day 110:

I Don't care How Tired You Are, There is No Greater Energy Than the Energy You Receive When You're Clocking Out of Work.

Day 111:

Younger men need us to be honest about

our flaws.

This helps guys feel safe about opening up and asking for help when

they need it.

Day 112:

Ironically, Most "Relationship Experts" Are Not In Relationships.

Day 113:

When You Are Down To NOTHING!

GOD Is Up To SOMETHING.

Day 114:

Encourage Your Self.

Day 115:

WHATEVER YOU ARE BE A GREAT ONE!

Day 116:

Avoid people who claim that everything wrong with them is someone else's fault!

Day 117:

Remember me in your prayers as you do in your gossip!

Day 118:

This is the day that the lord has made, let us rejoice and be glad in it.

Day 119:

PRAY FOR YOURSELF!

Day 120:

Thank You Lord For Blessing Me Much More Then I Deserve.

Day 121:

I Love to see people working in their purpose and passion.

Day 122:

There are things we don't want to happen but have to accept. Things we don't want to know but have to learn. And people we can't live without but have to let go.

Day 123:

Today I pray for those who need a turnaround in their Job, Finances, or Relationship. GOD can make all things NEW.

Day 124:

GOD IS GOING TO EXCEED YOUR EXPECTATIONS!

Day 125:

Sending Love To Everyone Who is Trying Their Best To Heal From Things That They Don't Discuss.

Day 126:

Sometimes We Don't Know What GOD Is Doing. The Key Is, Just Let Him Do It.

Day 127:

Never Ruin An Apology With An Excuse.

Day 128:

Faith Is Like Wi-Fi

It's Invisible,

But

It Has The Power

To Connect You

To

What You Need.

Day 129:

I Hope You Always Find A Reason To Smile.

Day 130:

Every Day May Not Be Good, But There is Something Good In Every Day.

Day 131:

small

Changes Can Make

a

BIG

Difference

Day 132:

GOD, You Saved Me From The Very Things That Have Killed Other People.

THANK YOU, GOD!

Day 133:

You Can't Make Somebody Act Right, But You Can Make Them Wish They Did.

Day 134:

Your Time Line Could Be Someone's Lifeline.

Encourage Someone Today.

Day 135:

I AM NOT A PASTOR.

I JUST LOVE TALKING ABOUT JESUS!

Day 136:

GOD Can Turn Broken Pieces Into Masterpieces.

Day 137:

Instead of Moving Out of the Hood, Let's Make the Hood What We Desire It to Be!

Day 138:

PRAY

FOR

ME!

Day 139:

A CHILD SHOULD NOT HAVE

TO

BEG A PARENT FOR

A RELATIONSHIP!

Day 140:

Some Of Your "Friends" Like You Better Broken.

STOP

Over-Looking What You See.

You Notice it!

Day 141:

SUPPORT YOUR FAMILY AND FRIENDS LIKE YOU DO THESE CELEBRITIES!

Day 142:

A LOT OF PEOPLE HAVE THE WRONG IDEA

ABOUT ME

AND

I HAVE NO DESIRE TO CLEAR IT UP!

Day 143:

NOT All STORMS COME TO DISRUPT YOUR LIFE,

SOME COME TO CLEAR YOUR PATH!

Day 144:

Whether You Think You Can, Or Think You Can't, You are Probably Right!

Day 145:

Start venting to God.

He's not going to tell a soul.

Day 146:

Never Look Down On Anyone.

Only GOD Sits That High.

Day 147:

If You Cannot Be Positive, Then At Least Be Quiet.

Day 148:

DON'T LET WHAT YOU SEE, MAKE YOU FORGET WHAT I SAID!

-GOD

Day 149:

It's not that they don't like what you're doing, they don't like that it's you doing it.

Day 150:

Look for someone who will work with you to get it.

Not someone who will work at getting you because you got it.

Day 151:

Hurt People
Hurt People
But
Healed People
Heal People.

Day 152:

As a people, you can't just have any person representing you. They have to be solid. If they are a clown, you'll look like a clown too. They have to know and understand that.

Day 153:

I PRAY,

THAT EVERY STUDENT SUCCESSFULLY MAKES IT THROUGH SCHOOL, UNHARMED AND SAFE THIS YEAR!

Day 154:

When you don't move into your purpose, you don't move into the total power of God for your life.

Day 155:

It's ok to be angry. It's just not ok to do something stupid when you're angry.

Think Twice!

Restrain!

Wisdom!

Day 156:

Stop worrying about what people "think" so much. Most of them change their mind by tomorrow anyway.

No Worries!

Day 157:

P.U.S.H.E.D

PRAY

UNTIL

SOMETHING

HAPPENS

EVERY

DAY!

Day 158:

Ain't no room for negotiations when it comes to RESPECT.

Day 159:

Do you love them enough to wait until they become who they are supposed to be? Now let that sink in for a second.

Day 160:

(LADIES)

So your friend never asks you if your kids are hungry?

Only if they are asleep.

Day 161:

I'll get Inspired before I get jealous.

Day 162:

"I CAN'T WAIT UNTIL I'M GROWN,"

Was the dumbest thing I've ever said.

Day 163:

Love is not

seeing

how much stuff

you can take from

another

person.

Day 164:

Don't Be Fooled, People Aren't Who They "Post" To Be.

Day 165:

YOU CAN'T BUILD WITH SOMEONE WHO EXPECTS YOU TO DO ALL THE WORK!

Day 166:

When a child is learning how to walk and falls down 50 times, they never think to themselves, "Maybe this isn't for me."

Day 167:

Love

Is A

Sacrifice.

Day 168:

Stay focused.

Follow

ones

course

until

successful

every day.

Day 169:

Extinction is the Rule.

Survival is the Exception.

Day 170:

(STUPID)

Knowing The Truth,

Seeing The Truth, But Still Believing A Lie.

Don't Be STUPID!

Day 171:

Grab a plate and throw it on the ground.

-Okay, done.

Did it break?

-Yes.

Now, say sorry for it.

-Sorry.

Did it go back to the way it was before?

-No.

Do You Understand?

Day 172:

FINISH THIS SENTENCE:

To Better Improve My Quality Of Life, I Need To

__________________.

Day 173:

Some People Just Act Like They Are Trying To Help You.

Day 174:

The Best Way

To

Find Love Is

To

Find GOD.

Day 175: Hustle Until Your Haters Ask If You're Hiring.

Day 176:

One Of The Signs Of Maturity Is Your Ability To See What's Wrong With You.

Day 177:

Try To Hang Around People Who Believe In You Or Support You.

Sometimes That's Nobody.

Day 178:

You Don't Really Know Someone Until You Fight Them.

Day 179:

It's A Privilege To Learn About Racism Instead Of Experiencing It Your Whole Life.

Day 180:

Don't Cling To A Mistake Just Because You Spent A Lot Of Time Making It.

Day 181:

You Can't Be Given Freedom. You Have To Take It.

Day 182:

Sometimes People Pretend

To Be

Your Friend

To

Get Things From You.

Day 183:

JUST BECAUSE YOU ARE OFFENDED, THAT DOESN'T MEAN THAT YOU ARE RIGHT!

Day 184:

Imagine Taking Someone For Granted And Then Never Finding Anyone Like Them Again.

Day 185:

You're Not

A

Second Option, They Will Either Choose You

Or

Lose You.

Day 186:

If They Left You Without A Reason, They Cannot Come Back With An Excuse.

Day 187:

Sometimes It's Not What You Say That Matters, It's What You Don't. #ACTION

Day 188:

Make Sure YOU LOVE YOURSELF FIRST, Before YOU Enter A RELATIONSHIP, Because That's Really WHO YOU Will Be Spending The Rest Of Your Life With.

Day 189:

Straight Roads Do Not Make Skillful Drivers.

Day 190:

Be Loyal Behind My Back.

Day 191:

Life Never Stops Teaching.

So Always Keep Learning.

Day 192:

The Biggest Slap to your Enemies Is Your Success.

Day 193:

Never Lower Your Standards For A Person.

Make Them Raise Their Standards For You.

Day 194:

A Relationship Is A Privilege, Not A Chore.

Love Should Be Appreciated, Not Taken For Granted.

Day 195:

Learn To Appreciate What You Have Before Time Makes You Appreciate What You Had.

Day 196:

GOD TOLD ME TO TELL YOU

TO

STAY OUT OF

MY

BUSINESS!

Day 197:

Marriage is a Ministry.

If YOU are not ready to labor in prayer, be faithful & get rid of selfishness, do not apply for that position.

Day 198:

Y'all Do Know There's Enough Room For ALL of US to Win, Right?

Day 199:

Some Of Ya'll are Playing Hide & Seek With Jesus.

PRETTY SOON HE'S GONNA SAY, "READY OR NOT HERE I COME!"

Day 200:

When Life Gets Blurry, Adjust Your Focus.

Day 201:

LOVE IS DEAF!

YOU CAN'T JUST TELL SOMEONE YOU LOVE THEM,

YOU HAVE TO SHOW THEM!

Day 202:

YOU DESERVE WHAT YOU SETTLE FOR!

Day 203:

How They Treat You

Is How They Feel About

You.

Day 204:

PEOPLE

Will Really Be Mad

At You

For Knowing

Your

Worth.

Day 205:

Surround Yourself With PEOPLE That Feed Your Soul, Not Eat It.

Day 206:

The same red flags

you ignore

in the beginning

of a relationship,

will most likely

be

the same

reason that it

ends.

Day 207:

WHEN I FOUND MYSELF, I FOUND MY SOUL MATE!

Day 208:

If It Costs You Your PEACE, It's Too Expensive.

Day 209:

When you say

YES

to others,

make sure you are not saying

NO

to yourself.

Day 210:

Negative People Need Drama Like Oxygen.

Stay Positive, It Will Take Their Breath Away.

Day 211:

The Happiest People Don't Have The Best Of Everything. They Make The Best Of Everything

Day 212:

The Majority Of People Can Hear But Have No Clue On How To Listen.

Day 213:

Stop trying to tell people what to do with the hurt

YOU

gave them.

They'll never be wrong about how

YOU

made them feel.

Day 214:

I Don't Forgive People Because I'm Weak, I Forgive People Because I'M STRONG Enough TO Know That People Make Mistakes.

Day 215:

I WILL Forgive you, But I WILL NOT Forget How YOU Made ME FEEL.

Day 216:

Whatever You Do, Never Run Back To What Broke You.

Day 217:

Honesty Is A Very Expensive Gift. Don't Expect It From Cheap People.

Day 218:

STOP GIVING THE SAME PERSON, DIFFERENT OPPORTUNITIES TO DISAPPOINT YOU!

Day 219:

I AM MY ANCESTORS' WILDEST DREAMS.

Day 220:

I don't think You Understand, Everything Was Impossible Until Someone did it. The Word itself Broken Down says IM-POSSIBLE.

Day 221:

My Circle got so small, it's a Period.

Day 222:

I asked God to help me grow And it started raining!

Day 223:

Stop Changing Who You Are For People Who Don't Even Know Themselves.

Day 224:

Some people just want to be Angry.

It has nothing to do with you.

Day 225:

Social media NEEDS TO SHUT DOWN FOR A YEAR SO PEOPLE CAN GO BACK TO BEING THEMSELVES

Day 226:

GOD FORGIVE ME IF I ASKED YOU MORE THAN I THANKED YOU!

Day 227:

I Want To Be An Actor and Motivational Speaker.

GOD Wants me to be a Man of God, who loves being a Husband, Father, Teacher, Author, and Entrepreneur. #GodFirst

Day 228:

Jealousy Will Have You Gossiping About Who You Should Be Learning From.

Day 229:

First It Hurts. Then It Changes You.

Day 230:

Marriage flourishes when the couple works together as a team. When both husband and wife decide that winning together is more important than keeping score.

Day 231:

Sometimes in life we have to slow down. I got on this path I created and wanted to run it down. However, HE said slow down and walk with me. You don't have to run from anything I AM making YOU!

Day 232:

Knowledge Speaks, But Wisdom Listens.

We can only know that we know nothing.

And that is the highest degree of human wisdom.

Day 233:

GOD IS FOR US!

Day 234:

If You Really Love Someone It Never Goes Away, Although You May Never Relive The Situation or Scenario. You Will Always Want The Best For Them No Matter What.

Day 235:

Your relationship with yourself sets the tone for every other relationship you have.

Day 236:

I understood myself only after I destroyed myself.

And only in the process of fixing myself, did I know who I really was.

Day 237:

You have the power to reshape and redefine any experience, no matter how devastating it seems.

Day 238:

Get alone, have your quiet time and search your heart. Say, "God, anything I've pushed down, anything that I've given up on, show me what it is. God, don't let me die with my dreams still buried."

Day 239:

Sometimes when you're feeling overwhelmed the answer may be to loosen your grip & consider what you're holding back out of fear & insecurity. You can be at rest because the Lord Himself fights your battles

Day 240:

No Hating Has Ever Stopped Me From Getting It.

Day 241:

In Order To Mold His People, God Often Has To Melt Them.

Day 242:

Hardship often prepares an ordinary person for an extraordinary destiny.

Day 243:

Marriage Is A Partnership Of Three. God, Husband And Wife.

Day 244:

Beauty Begins The Moment You Decide To Be Yourself.

Day 245:

Most Folks Are About As Happy As They Make Up Their Minds To Be.

Day 246:

When Your Work Speaks For Itself, Don't Interrupt.

Day 247:

Wake up every morning and be thankful for the spouse you have. Someone is praying for a spouse just like the one you have.

Day 248:

Falling Down Is How We Grow!

Staying Down Is How We Die!

Day 249:

Every day may not be good, but there's something good in every day.

Day 250:

I Pray That Whoever Reads This, God Heals Whatever Is Hurting You.

Day 251:

Have you Ever Wondered Why People Sit Back And Really Try And Hurt You?

It's Because You Let Them.

Day 252:

I Didn't Go To Ivy League schools, But The People Who Work For Me Did.

Day 253:

I DON'T KNOW WHO NEEDS TO HEAR THIS, BUT GOD IS THE PLUG!

Day 254:

So many sad people with happy pictures.

Day 255:

You can't be bitter and expect a sweet life.

Day 256:

"I LOVE YOU," DOESN'T LOOK LIKE WHAT MOST OF YOU THINK IT LOOKS LIKE!

Day 257:

IT'S THE START, THAT STOPS MOST PEOPLE!

Day 258:

IF YOU CAN CHANGE YOUR MIND,

YOU CAN CHANGE YOUR LIFE!

Day 259:

IF YOU DIDN'T HEAR IT WITH YOUR OWN EARS OR SEE IT WITH YOUR EYES, DON'T INVENT IT WITH YOUR SMALL MIND AND SHARE IT WITH YOUR BIG MOUTH!

Day 260:

The person who challenges you and holds you accountable loves you more than those who watch you stay the same and settle for mediocrity.

Day 261:

Your own family will talk stuff about you when you're in the process of breaking all their generational curses.

This ain't for the weak.

Day 262:

For The Record,

I Don't Need

You

To Believe In Me

To Get It Done.

Day 263:

No One Really Gives Anymore! They All Want What They Can Get Instead.

Day 264:

If It Doesn't Challenge YOU, It Won't Change You.

Day 265:

If YOU Entertain A Clown, YOU Become A Part Of The Circus!

Day 266:

I can't stand an always positive person,

walking around all day being positive.

Who does that?

Day 267:

If GOD Can Do Anything For Anybody, GOD Can Do Something For YOU.

Day 268:

Your relationship with yourself sets the tone for every other relationship that you have.

Day 269:

I understood myself, only after I destroyed myself. And only in the process of fixing myself, did I know who I really was.

Day 270:

You have the power to reshape and redefine any experience, no matter how devastating it seems.

Day 271:

Get alone, have your quiet time, and search your heart. Say, "God, anything I've pushed down, anything that I've given up on, show me what it is. God, don't let me die with my dreams still buried."

DAY 272:

What Other People Think Of Me Is None Of My Business.

DAY 273:

The Difference Between Greatness And Mediocrity Is The Small Things.

Be Effective In The Details.

DAY 274:

The enemy would love for you to go around feeling unworthy like you don't deserve to be blessed because you don't perform perfectly. Don't believe those lies. Who you are, never changes. You are still a child of God.

DAY 275:

You may have had an unfair past, but you don't have to have an unfair future. You may have gotten off to a rough start in life, but it's not how you start that matters. It's how you finish.

DAY 276:

If you don't speak up, you will never be heard.

DAY 277:

Love says,

"I am going to do this for you because I want to do this for you."

It doesn't say,

"if you do this for me, I'll do this for you."

DAY 278:

My Prayer To God Has Always Been, USE ME LORD To Motivate, Inspire, And Encourage Your People, All People.

DAY 279:

Disobedience kills your sacrifice and sometimes people do the right thing for the wrong reasons, without a true heart of good intentions.

DAY 280:

You Don't Want To Die.

You Just Want To Stop Hurting.

I Speak Life To You Now.

In Jesus' Name!

DAY 281:

Sometimes, the thing that breaks your Heart clears your vision.

DAY 282:

Your strength won't be attractive to everybody, but you better not shrink.

DAY 283:

Learn to Work Through Your Differences with Patience and Love.

DAY 284:

The Truth Is, Everybody's Going To Hurt You.

DAY 285:

A Negative Mind Will Never Give You A Positive Life.

DAY 286:

Lord, If You Don't Do Anything Else For Me, Thank You For All That You Have Done.

DAY 287:

Some people are holding serious grudges against you over stuff they did.

DAY 288:

Every Decision Has Its Consequences Or Blessings. Could Be Both!

Day 289:

You're Not Hurting Me, You're Hurting Yourself.

Day 290:

People Will Feel Some Type of Way Towards You And Let Everyone Know except You.

Day 291:

One Day When The Right Person Comes Into Your Life, You Will Understand Why The Wrong Person Had To Leave.

Day 292:

We Are Living In A World Where Man Doesn't Understand The Value Of Good Women And How Good Women Could Help Him Become Great.

Day 293:

There comes a time in your life, when you walk away from all the drama and people who create it. You surround yourself with people who make you laugh. Forget the bad and focus on the good.

Love the people who treat you right and pray for those who don't. Life is too short to be anything but happy. Falling down is a part of life. Getting back up is Living.

Day 294:

Where you are is not where you have to stay. God is called El Shaddai—the God of more than enough. He's not the God of barely enough. He's not the God of, just help me to make it through. He's the

God of abundance, the God of overflow. You have to tell yourself, "I didn't come this far, only to come this far." Just know, Everything you are going through is preparing you for what you asked for.

Day 295:

I Pray That Whoever Reads This, God Heals Whatever Is Hurting You.

Day 296:

If you knew who you were, you wouldn't struggle to be who you are.

Day 297:

Wisdom is knowing what you want and what you need.

Happiness is knowing what you have to keep and what you have to let go.

Day 298:

I just realized I've never seen a commercial for Chinese Food in my Life.

Day 299:

I Had an Idea For Years And Had The Nerve to be Disturbed when I See Someone Else Make it Happen!

GOD told me that's my Fault.

Day 300:

I'm training myself to remain calm in every situation and not give emotional responses. Everything we experience in life, good or bad, is preparing us for our next phase.

Day 301:

There are things we have to learn and grasp before we can move forward, and as long as we choose not to learn them, the longer we'll stay neutral.

Day 302:

Recognize the lesson in each situation. Especially the bad ones, so you can learn, adapt quickly and move on.

Day 303:

There are major things ahead. Don't get side-tracked by the minor mishaps.

Day 304:

Passion is energy.

Feel the power

that

comes from

focusing on what

excites you.

Day 305:

**Formal education
will
make you a
living.
Self-education
will
make you a
fortune.**

Day 306:

AN UPGRADE IS NOT SOMEONE WHO LOOKS BETTER THAN YOUR LAST. AN UPGRADE IS SOMEONE WHO TREATS, APPRECIATES, AND VALUES YOU MORE THAN YOUR LAST!

Day 307:

God made me
stronger

last year,

He is making me
happy

this year.

Day 308:

PROTECT OUR KIDS, EVEN IF THEY'RE NOT YOURS!

Day 309:

If there is no

enemy within,

the

enemy outside

of us

can do us

no harm.

Day 310:

One of the greatest things I ever did was learn how to be my own friend

&

separate myself.

Day 311:

As soon as y'all wake up y'all go straight to

social media. Don't even know if ya'll are able

walk or not.

Day 312:

Just because a man holds a wrench, doesn't make him a mechanic. Just because a man wears a ring, doesn't make him a

HUSBAND!

Day 313:

Sometimes, God will expose how people really feel about you during a petty argument!

Day 314:

You can have it all.

Day 315:

GOD IS GOING TO EXCEED YOUR EXPECTATIONS!

DAY 316:

You did not marry an angel. Every marriage is made up of two sinners. Regardless of how hard your spouse tries to be good, they will disappoint, hurt or frustrate you, repeatedly.

Therefore, don't expect your spouse to be a saint. Rather, enter marriage with a realistic expectation to be hurt and a readiness to forgive.

DAY 317:

Confidence is not "They will like me", confidence is "I'll be good even if they don't."

Day 318:

Prayer is not a button to be pushed,

it is a relationship to be pursued.

Day 319:

I SWEAR, DOING EVERYTHING ON YOUR OWN CAN BE VERY CHALLENGING AT TIMES, BUT THAT FEELING YOU HAVE WHEN YOU LOOK BACK AT HOW FAR YOU'VE ELEVATED,

KNOWING IT'S ALL BECAUSE OF YOU; PROUD DOESN'T BEGIN TO EXPLAIN IT!

Day 320:

When people check on YOU without wanting anything FROM you, you are blessed. Encouragement is one of the greatest gifts and I appreciate those who give it without motives.

Day 321:

Most people would rather be entertained than educated.

Day 322:

Be encouraged.

Be empowered.

God is removing

your burdens

And

bringing

you

major blessings.

Day 323:

I know Money

is the root to

all evil

but

Attention has to

be close.

Day 324:

No one is OBLIGATED to HELP your GROWN self.

Day 325:

I thank God for knowing me inside and out.

Day 326:

If you are broke because you pay your bills, you are not broke, you are responsible.

Day 327:

STRENGTH doesn't come from what you CAN do. It comes from the things you've overcome and thought you COULDN'T do.

Day 328:

A lot of people don't usually love a person until they're gone. Then, it's too late.

DAY 329:

And when you can't hear My voice,

please

trust my plan.

Day 330:

How They Treat You Is

How They

Feel About You.

People Aren't Out Here Mistreating You

On An Accident.

Day 331:

One Thing I've Learned About Life is: It Goes On.

Day 332:

How

is

Your Soul?

Day 333:

When a toxic person can no longer control you, they will try to control how others see you. The misinformation will feel unfair but stay above it. Trust that other people will eventually see the TRUTH, just like you did.

Day 334:

Be Thankful for what you have, and you will end up having more.

If you concentrate on what you don't have, you will never ever have enough.

Day 335:

GOD Will Answer Your Prayer When You Stop Worshiping It.

Day 336:

God never gives you a dream that matches your budget.

He is not checking your bank account.

He is checking your faith.

Day 337:

God, please

give me the

strength

to remove anyone

who is

using me,

hurting me,

and

toxic for me.

Day 338:

Today I will engage in the art of strategic silence. I believe God can show more than I can ever SAY.

Sometimes we give the enemy too much to work with by

saying something we shouldn't say. Have an awesome day!

Day 339:

STRONG PEOPLE DON'T HAVE TO SAY THEY'RE STRONG, THEY JUST DEMONSTRATE IT!

Day 340:

Have you ever ASKED A person for NOTHING,

and

they

STILL DIDN'T HAVE IT.

Day 341:

Many will never get what they desire because they don't know how to master their dialogue. Stop sharing thoughts, ideas, plans, frustrations, displeasure, etc.

The enemy is mentally illiterate (he can't read minds). So he only works with what you say. With that being said, let your results make the loudest noise.

Day 342:

You all better stop disliking people over what you heard,

and

be thankful God isn't disliking you over what He knows.

DAY 343:

BE INTO YOUR SELF!

DAY 344:

DON'T EVER FORGET HOW TO SMILE!

DAY 345:

MAKE AN O.A.T.H

OVERCOMING ADVERSITY THROUGH HUMILITY!

DAY 346:

YOU MAY SEE ME STRUGGLE BUT YOU WILL NEVER SEE ME QUIT!

Day 347:

Hurt In Private.

Heal In Private.

Shine In Public.

Day 348:

EVERY RELATIONSHIP SHOULD TEACH YOU SOMETHING. THEY WILL TEACH YOU HOW YOU ARE SUPPOSED TO BE TREATED OR HOW THE GAMES ARE PLAYED!

Day 349:

You would be surprised who is jealous of whom. They don't even have to have anything.

Day 350:

What Happens,

Is

Not As

Important

As How

You React

To

What Happens.

DAY 351:

Thank You, GOD, for Everything, I mean, EVERYTHING.

DAY 352:

GOD RESTORES THE BROKEN!

DAY 353:

God

I pray that you cause me to meet Great success in You

A Surplus of Prosperity

It is my season

DAY 354:

When you look at a Person,

Any Person.

Remember that Everyone has a Story.

Everyone has gone through something that has changed them.

L.I.F.E

LEADING INDIVIDUALS THROUGH THE FOSTER CARE EXPERIENCE

DAY 355:

If you really want to do something, you will find a way If you don't, you will find an excuse.

DAY 356:

You don't get to choose

when or whom

you meet,

but you do get to choose

whom you hold on

to.

DAY 357:

At my Job, I help save Lives.

DAY 358:

Being happy does not mean everything is perfect. It means you have decided to look past the imperfections, which is a perfect feeling.

Day 359:

Life is a good thing, and I believe everyone should have one.

Day 360:

GOD

IS

LOVE!

Day 361:

Have no

F.E.A.R

False evidence appearing real.

Day 362:

Don't Lose Your Mind, and Keep Your Heart.

Day 363:

For What It's Worth,

It's Never Too Late To Be Whomever You Want To Be.

I Hope You Live A Life You're Proud Of.

And If You Find That You Are Not,

I Hope You Have The Strength To Start Over.

Day 364:

We always have the ability to learn.

refLect
solvE
creAte
gRow
thiNk

We just have to pay attention.

DAY 365:

He is,

The Alpha and Omega,

The beginning and the end.

Life can be a lot like school. You learn by listening and by asking questions. The people around you provide a tremendous resource. They have experiences and knowledge that you do not have. You have the opportunity to learn from them. If you have surrounded yourself with people who have no desire to grow or increase and are not interested in helping you in that pursuit; this is the time to evaluate your associations. Find people who can teach you. Ask questions. Then listen

closely to what they say. Seek to understand; make a goal to learn something new every day that will benefit you in reaching your goals and dreams. If you do this, you will be amazed at how much your mind will increase and your thinking will expand in just a few weeks. "Give a Man a Fish, and You will Feed Him for a Day. Teach a Man To Fish, and You will Feed Him for a Lifetime." #focused (follow ones course until successful everyday)

Works Cited

https://www.merriam-webster.com
https://www.bible.com
https://pt.scribd.com/book/401091660/Karma
http://forum.bodybuilding.com/showthread.php?t=89940
https://scholarship.shu.edu/yearbooks/46
http://forum.bodybuilding.com/showthread.php?t=89940
https://onsizzle.com/t/ledger
https://journeywithparkinsons.com/category/neurodegenerative-disorders/page/2/
http://benzaiten.dyndns.org/BarackObama/BarackObama_05677.html
https://mmaengage.com/anniversary-wishes-for-parents/good-morning-wishes-with-smile-quotes
http://benzaiten.dyndns.org/BarackObama/BarackObama_05027.html
https://www.wiseoldsayings.com/inner-strength-quotes/
https://liveinspiremotivate.com/author/live-inspire-motivate/
https://www.thefreshquotes.com/life-transforming-motivational-quotes-powerful-life-quotes/
https://pdfcoffee.com/the-treasury-of-quotes-3-pdf-free.html
http://epicquotes.org/view.php?id=1154&page=2
http://www.jimdavidsoncolumn.com/columns/all
https://me.me/t/queen-bee?s=new&since=1540478046%2Ca78725a4aa764de2b4ceb40ed8611243

https://me.me/t/heard?s=%F0%9F%94%A5&since=1566583474%2C5f7041c58e5744819be681c9239a89c0%2C0
https://me.me/t/c3po
https://ivy.fm/tag/confidence-tips
http://www.potomacag.org/utilities/file_library/documents/RoyalRangers/Tomahawk%20NovDec%202015.pdf
http://semurniikatankasih.blogspot.com/2011/12/
https://www.dailymail.co.uk/tvshowbiz/article-6626067/Khloe-Kardashian-posts-quote-having-nervous-breakdown-sharing-clips-baby-True.html
https://silo.pub/blessed-in-the-darkness.html
https://mmaengage.com/anniversary-wishes-for-parents/good-morning-wishes-with-smile-quotes
http://benzaiten.dyndns.org/BarackObama/BarackObama_05677.html
http://www.tips21.com/most-liked-facebook-status.html
https://pdfcoffee.com/the-treasury-of-quotes-3-pdf-free.html
https://www.marieforleo.com/blog/sheri-riley
https://me.me/t/dumbest-thing?s=new&since=1550601274%2C703b50b2ad004881ad4036eff82205fc
https://me.me/t/falls?s=%F0%9F%94%A5&since=1552007812%2C460ce1526d684c9ba8bd5729469f4e77%2C0
https://me.me/t/say-sorry?s=new&since=1576089971%2Ce69de1f0b6a6405ea7e1244b2a3fed53

https://www.gamified.uk/2021/05/26/confirmation-bias-and-how-to-embrace-being-wrong-ux/amp/

http://thequotesmaster.com/2017/11/awesome-facebook-statuses/

http://thequotesmaster.com/2017/11/awesome-facebook-statuses/

http://thequotesmaster.com/2017/11/awesome-facebook-statuses/

https://www.studymode.com/v1/turnitin_essay/772208

https://aldowningministries.org/ministery-blog/

http://thequotesmaster.com/2017/11/awesome-facebook-statuses/

http://thequotesmaster.com/2017/11/awesome-facebook-statuses/

https://www.searchquotes.com/quotes/about/Drama/2/

https://www.searchquotes.com/quotes/about/Drama/2/

http://www.skatewhat.com/russhowell/WebPage-Quotes-FloatingMenu.html

http://www.tips21.com/most-liked-facebook-status.html

https://me.me/t/honesty-is?s=new&since=1524537955%2C21497069

https://www.chronicle.co.zw/some-commendable-marriage-nuggets/

https://dpsayings.com/dreams-quotes-sayings/

https://sermons.love/joel-osteen/407-joel-osteen-remember-your-dream.html

http://www.skatewhat.com/russhowell/WebPage-Quotes-FloatingMenu.html

http://benzaiten.dyndns.org/BarackObama/BarackObama_05677.html
https://me.me/t/192475
http://www.goupstate.com/article/20120131/COLUMNISTS/201311003/0/FRONTPAGE?Title=The-Stroller-Term-limits-
http://loveyoulovegod.com/category/amy/
https://www.truthorfiction.com/did-denzel-washington-say-your-own-family-will-discredit-you-when-youre-breaking-generational-curses
http://www.skatewhat.com/russhowell/WebPage-Quotes-FloatingMenu.html
https://dpsayings.com/dreams-quotes-sayings/
https://sermons.love/joel-osteen/407-joel-osteen-remember-your-dream.html
http://www.jimdavidsoncolumn.com/columns/all
https://silo.pub/blessed-in-the-darkness.html
http://www.scottwimberly.com/let-go-2/
http://www.jimdavidsoncolumn.com/columns/all
https://www.blackhatworld.com
http://rebeccastevenson.blogspot.com/2011/07/
https://kennard1.typepad.com/blog/page/114/
https://dpsayings.com/dreams-quotes-sayings/
http://www.skatewhat.com/russhowell/WebPage-Quotes-FloatingMenu.html
https://phpc.social/@augustohp/media
http://tnoncology.com/blog/2017/11/24/thankful/
https://www.1cor619fit.com/about
https://me.me/t/heard?s=%F0%9F%94%A5&since=1566583474%2C5f7041c58e5744819be681c9239a89c0%2C

http://www.ccainstitute.org/our-programs/foster-youth-internship/wherearetheynow.html
https://scholarship.shu.edu/yearbooks/46
https://thomasloebmd.com/rhinoplasty/selfie-for-self-esteem-scholarship-award/
http://www.mandalaforchange.com/tag/courage/
https://journeywithparkinsons.com/category/neurodegenerative-disorders/page/2/
http://forum.bodybuilding.com/showthread.php?t=89940